Body Bugs

This bug looks big,
but really it's tiny.
The picture just makes it look big.
It is a dust mite,
and it feeds on bits of your body!

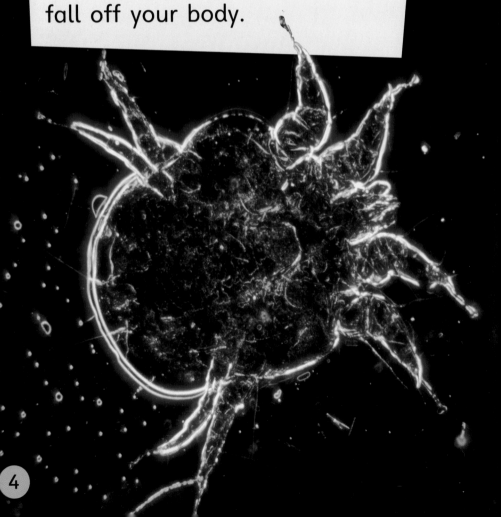

Tiny Mites

Over a million dust mites
live in your bed!
They are too tiny to see.
They eat bits of dead skin that
fall off your body.

BLOODSUCKERS

Contents

Haydn Middleton

Story illustrated by
Fitz Hammond

Before Reading

Find out about

- All the bugs that live on you, around you – or *inside* you!

Tricky words

- tiny
- million
- mouths
- crawl
- tapeworms
- thunderbugs
- midges

Introduce these tricky words and help the reader when they come across them later!

Text starter

Did you know that millions of tiny creatures like to eat *you*! Mites and fleas suck your blood and tapeworms can grow inside your stomach!

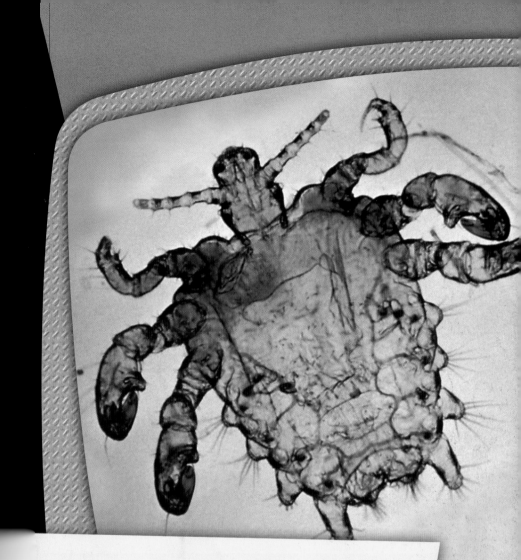

Some mites don't wait for the dead skin to fall off your body. They just dig into your body and start eating!

Fleas

Some dogs get fleas.
The fleas bite their skin
and suck their blood.

But fleas can jump over 30 cms.
So they can jump from a dog
on to you!

Then the fleas feed on you.
They bite your skin with their
sharp, little mouths.
Then they suck your blood.

Lice

Body lice live in really dirty clothes.

Then they crawl on to **you!**

They like sucking your blood.

Head lice live in your hair. They like clean hair better than dirty hair. They crawl along your hair – then they bite your head and suck your blood!

Worms

People can get worms growing inside them!

If you eat food that is not cooked well, the bugs in the food are still alive. Then the bugs become worms in your tummy.

A tapeworm looks like a long piece of flat spaghetti.

Tapeworms can grow really long inside you. Some can be up to 10m! They can live in your body for up to 30 years!

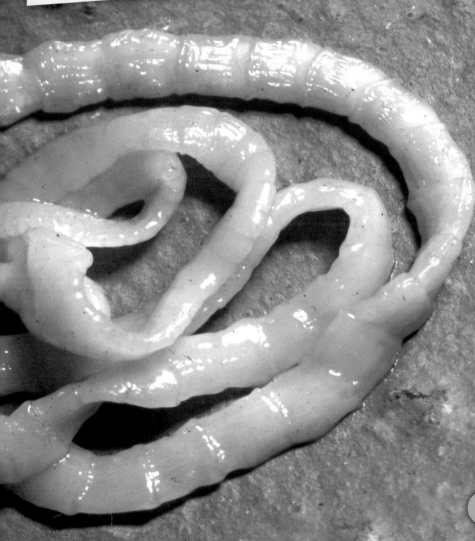

Flying Bugs

Thunderbugs are tiny flying bugs.
They fly around on hot days.
You can feel them on your skin.
But they don't want your blood.
They just like to *crawl* all over
your body!

Some bugs **do** want your blood.
Midges fly at you – then they bite
and suck your blood.
But only *female* midges suck
your blood. They want your blood
because it helps their eggs to grow.

Male midges just
feed on flowers.

So look out!

Lots of bugs live on your body and like to eat you.

Quiz

Text Detective

- What do dust mites eat?
- Which fact do you think is the most disgusting?

Word Detective

- **Phonic Focus:** Long vowels
  Page 7: Sound out the phonemes (sounds) in 'feed'.
  What long vowel can you hear?
- Page 7: Find two words describing the fleas' mouths.
- Page 10: How many sentences are on this page?

Super Speller

Read these words:

grow   start   along

Now try to spell them!

HA! HA! HA!

Q What's smaller than an insect's mouth?

A Anything that it eats!

15

Before Reading

In this story

 Sam

 Sam's mum

 Sam's dog, Biff

 The fleas

Tricky words

- suddenly
- biting
- blood
- shrank
- happened
- tiny
- closer
- feast
- squashed

Introduce these tricky words and help the reader when they come across them later!

Story starter

Whenever Sam's mum asks Sam to do a *little* job, he shrinks! One day, Sam's mum asked him to get rid of the fleas that were biting Biff.

Shrinking Sam
and the
Fleas

Sam and his mum were in the park
with their dog, Biff.
Suddenly Biff jumped.
Then he jumped again.

"Oh no!" said Sam's mum.
"Biff's got fleas! They're biting him
to suck his blood. That's why
he's jumping!"

"Do a little job for me,"
said Sam's mum.
"Please take Biff to the vet
and get rid of those fleas."
She gave Sam some money.
"See you later!" she said.

Sam knew what would happen next.
There was a great big **FLASH**
and Sam shrank!
This always happened when his mum
asked him to do a *little* job.
Now Sam was tiny!

Biff sniffed the tiny Sam.
Sam jumped up on to Biff.
He **had** to get rid of the fleas.
Then he would grow to the
right size again.
But how could he do it?

Biff jumped again.

The fleas were biting him.

"*I'll* get rid of those fleas," Sam said.

"I'll kick them off."

Then he *saw* the fleas.

There were so many of them! And they were so big and full of blood that Sam could not kick them off.

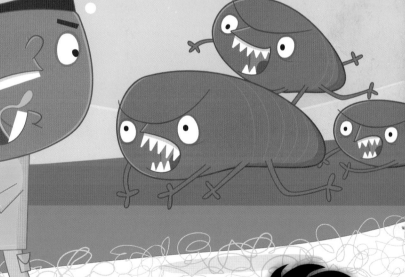

Is Sam happy to see the fleas?

The fleas looked at Sam.

They came closer and closer.

"Mmmmmm," they said.

"Fresh blood!"

Just then Sam saw a dirty stray dog.
It was the sort of dog that fleas
love to feed on.
Suddenly Sam had a great idea.

He said to the fleas,
"There's a real feast for you
over there!"
Sam showed the fleas the
stray dog.
"Mmmmm," said the fleas.
"But how can we get there?"

Sam said to Biff,

"Go and stand next to that dog."

Biff walked over to the stray dog.

"OK, fleas!" Sam shouted. "Jump!"
The fleas all jumped on to the
stray dog.
"Now *run*, Biff!" said Sam.

Biff ran and ... **_FLASH_**

Sam was the right size again.
But he was still on Biff's back,
and Biff was squashed flat!

Sam and Biff walked home.

"That was quick," said Sam's mum.

"Did you get rid of Biff's fleas?"

"I did," said Sam.

"And I did it for free!"

Quiz

- Why did Sam have to get rid of the fleas?
- What was Sam's great idea?

Word Detective

- Phonic Focus: Long vowels
  Page 29: Sound out the phonemes (sounds) in 'right'.
  What long vowel can you hear?
- Page 24: What do the fleas say?
- Page 28: Find a word that means 'called loudly'.

Super Speller

Read these words:

right   little   many

Now try to spell them!

HA! HA! HA!

 How do you start a flea race?

A One ... two ... flea ... go!